2OI9

SHAKES-

PLANNER

52 WEEKS OF THE BARD

BY

PLAY ON WORDS DESIGN

NOTES TO THY SELF:

NOTES TO THY SELF:

NOTES TO THY SELF:

NOTES TO THY SELF:

To be, or not to be: that is the question.

JANUARY

MONDAY

31

NEW YEAR'S EVE

TUESDAY

1

NEW YEAR'S DAY

WEDNESDAY

2

THURSDAY

3

FRIDAY

4

SATURDAY/SUNDAY

5/6

ALL THE WORLD'S A STAGE,
AND ALL THE MEN AND WOMEN
MERELY PLAYERS.

JANUARY

MONDAY	**7**
TUESDAY	**8**
WEDNESDAY	**9**
THURSDAY	**10**
FRIDAY	**11**
SATURDAY/SUNDAY	**12/13**

NOW IS THE WINTER OF OUR DISCONTENT.

JANUARY

MONDAY	**14**
TUESDAY	**15**
WEDNESDAY	**16**
THURSDAY	**17**
FRIDAY	**18**
SATURDAY/SUNDAY	**19/20**

Some are born great, some achieve greatness, and some have greatness thrust upon them.

JANUARY

MONDAY

21

MARTIN LUTHER KING JR. DAY

TUESDAY

22

WEDNESDAY

23

THURSDAY

24

FRIDAY

25

SATURDAY/SUNDAY

26/27

FRAILTY, THY NAME IS WOMAN.

JANUARY/FEBRUARY

MONDAY

28

TUESDAY

29

WEDNESDAY

30

THURSDAY

31

FRIDAY

1

SATURDAY/SUNDAY

2/3

GROUNDHOG DAY

IF YOU PRICK US, DO WE NOT BLEED? IF YOU TICKLE US, DO WE NOT LAUGH? IF YOU POISON US, DO WE NOT DIE? AND IF YOU WRONG US, SHALL WE NOT REVENGE?

FEBRUARY

MONDAY

4

TUESDAY

5

WEDNESDAY

6

THURSDAY

7

FRIDAY

8

SATURDAY/SUNDAY

9/10

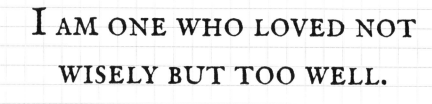

I AM ONE WHO LOVED NOT
WISELY BUT TOO WELL.

FEBRUARY

MONDAY

11

TUESDAY

12

WEDNESDAY

13

THURSDAY

14

VALENTINE'S DAY

FRIDAY

15

SATURDAY/SUNDAY

16/17

THE LADY DOTH PROTEST TOO MUCH.

FEBRUARY

MONDAY

18

PRESIDENTS DAY

TUESDAY

19

WEDNESDAY

20

THURSDAY

21

FRIDAY

22

SATURDAY/SUNDAY

23/24

WE ARE SUCH STUFF AS DREAMS ARE MADE ON.

FEBRUARY/MARCH

MONDAY
25

TUESDAY
26

WEDNESDAY
27

THURSDAY
28

FRIDAY
1

SATURDAY/SUNDAY
2/3

Exit, Pursued by a bear.

MARCH

MONDAY

4

TUESDAY

5

WEDNESDAY

6

THURSDAY

7

FRIDAY

8

SATURDAY/SUNDAY

9/10

BEWARE THE IDES OF MARCH.

MARCH

MONDAY

11

TUESDAY

12

WEDNESDAY

13

THURSDAY

14

FRIDAY

15

SATURDAY/SUNDAY

16/17

ST. PATRICK'S DAY

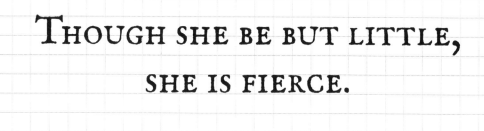

THOUGH SHE BE BUT LITTLE, SHE IS FIERCE.

MARCH

MONDAY	**18**
TUESDAY	**19**
WEDNESDAY	**20**
THURSDAY	**21**
FRIDAY	**22**
SATURDAY/SUNDAY	**23/24**

By the pricking of my thumbs, something wicked this way comes.

MARCH

MONDAY **25**

TUESDAY **26**

WEDNESDAY **27**

THURSDAY **28**

FRIDAY **29**

SATURDAY/SUNDAY **30/31**

DOUBLE, DOUBLE, TOIL AND TROUBLE.

APRIL

MONDAY

1

APRIL FOOL'S DAY

TUESDAY

2

WEDNESDAY

3

THURSDAY

4

FRIDAY

5

SATURDAY/SUNDAY

6/7

OUT, DAMNED SPOT!

APRIL

MONDAY

8

TUESDAY

9

WEDNESDAY

10

THURSDAY

11

FRIDAY

12

SATURDAY/SUNDAY

13/14

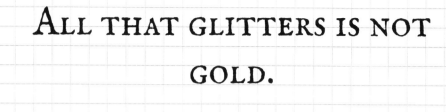

ALL THAT GLITTERS IS NOT GOLD.

APRIL

MONDAY
15

TUESDAY
16

WEDNESDAY
17

THURSDAY
18

FRIDAY
19

SATURDAY/SUNDAY
20/21
EASTER

TO THINE OWN SELF, BE TRUE.

APRIL

MONDAY

22

TUESDAY

23

SHAKESPEARE'S BIRTHDAY

WEDNESDAY

24

THURSDAY

25

FRIDAY

26

SATURDAY/SUNDAY

27/28

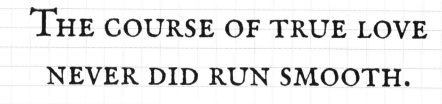

THE COURSE OF TRUE LOVE
NEVER DID RUN SMOOTH.

APRIL/MAY

MONDAY

29

TUESDAY

30

WEDNESDAY

1

THURSDAY

2

FRIDAY

3

SATURDAY/SUNDAY

4/5

CINCO DE MAYO

But soft, what light through yonder window breaks?

MAY

MONDAY

6

TUESDAY

7

WEDNESDAY

8

THURSDAY

9

FRIDAY

10

SATURDAY/SUNDAY

11/12

MOTHER'S DAY

WHAT'S IN A NAME? THAT WHICH WE CALL A ROSE BY ANY OTHER WORD WOULD SMELL AS SWEET.

MAY

MONDAY	**13**
TUESDAY	**14**
WEDNESDAY	**15**
THURSDAY	**16**
FRIDAY	**17**
SATURDAY/SUNDAY	**18/19**

I am constant as the Northern Star

MAY

MONDAY

20

TUESDAY

21

WEDNESDAY

22

THURSDAY

23

FRIDAY

24

SATURDAY/SUNDAY

25/26

ET TU, BRUTE?

MAY/JUNE

MONDAY

27

MEMORIAL DAY

TUESDAY

28

WEDNESDAY

29

THURSDAY

30

FRIDAY

31

SATURDAY/SUNDAY

1/2

MORE OF YOUR CONVERSATION WOULD INFECT MY BRAIN.

JUNE

MONDAY 3

TUESDAY 4

WEDNESDAY 5

THURSDAY 6

FRIDAY 7

SATURDAY/SUNDAY 8/9

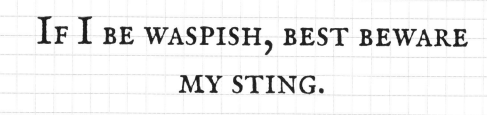

IF I BE WASPISH, BEST BEWARE MY STING.

JUNE

MONDAY 10

TUESDAY 11

WEDNESDAY 12

THURSDAY 13

FRIDAY 14

FLAG DAY

SATURDAY/SUNDAY 15/16

FATHER'S DAY

THE FOOL DOTH THINK HE IS
WISE, BUT THE WISE MAN KNOWS
HIMSELF TO BE A FOOL.

JUNE

MONDAY 17

TUESDAY 18

WEDNESDAY 19

THURSDAY 20

FRIDAY 21

SATURDAY/SUNDAY 22/23

SWEET ARE THE USES OF ADVERSITY.

JUNE

MONDAY 24

TUESDAY 25

WEDNESDAY 26

THURSDAY 27

FRIDAY 28

SATURDAY/SUNDAY 29/30

O WONDERFUL, WONDERFUL,
AND MOST WONDERFUL
WONDERFUL, AND YET AGAIN
WONDERFUL.

JULY

MONDAY

1

TUESDAY

2

WEDNESDAY

3

THURSDAY

4

INDEPENDENCE DAY

FRIDAY

5

SATURDAY/SUNDAY

6/7

AND THEREBY HANGS A TALE.

JULY

MONDAY **8**

TUESDAY **9**

WEDNESDAY **10**

THURSDAY **11**

FRIDAY **12**

SATURDAY/SUNDAY **13/14**

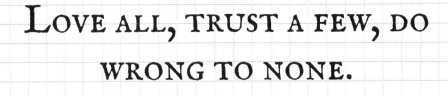

Love all, trust a few, do wrong to none.

JULY

MONDAY

15

TUESDAY

16

WEDNESDAY

17

THURSDAY

18

FRIDAY

19

SATURDAY/SUNDAY

20/21

So full of artless jealousy is guilt.

JULY

MONDAY

22

TUESDAY

23

WEDNESDAY

24

THURSDAY

25

FRIDAY

26

SATURDAY/SUNDAY

27/28

FAIR IS FOUL, AND FOUL IS FAIR.

JULY/AUGUST

MONDAY

29

TUESDAY

30

WEDNESDAY

31

THURSDAY

1

FRIDAY

2

SATURDAY/SUNDAY

3/4

THE FIRST THING WE DO, LET'S KILL ALL THE LAWYERS.

AUGUST

MONDAY 5

TUESDAY 6

WEDNESDAY 7

THURSDAY 8

FRIDAY 9

SATURDAY/SUNDAY 10/11

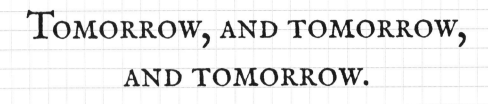

Tomorrow, and tomorrow, and tomorrow.

AUGUST

MONDAY 12

TUESDAY 13

WEDNESDAY 14

THURSDAY 15

FRIDAY 16

SATURDAY/SUNDAY 17/18

It is a tale told by an idiot, full of sound and fury, signifying nothing.

AUGUST

MONDAY 19

TUESDAY 20

WEDNESDAY 21

THURSDAY 22

FRIDAY 23

SATURDAY/SUNDAY 24/25

TO SLEEP, PERCHANCE TO DREAM.

AUGUST/SEPTEMBER

MONDAY

26

TUESDAY

27

WEDNESDAY

28

THURSDAY

29

FRIDAY

30

SATURDAY/SUNDAY

31/1

WELL SAID, OLD MOLE!

SEPTEMBER

MONDAY

2

LABOR DAY

TUESDAY

3

WEDNESDAY

4

THURSDAY

5

FRIDAY

6

SATURDAY/SUNDAY

7/8

THERE ARE MORE THINGS IN HEAVEN AND EARTH, HORATIO, THAN ARE DREAMT OF IN YOUR PHILOSOPHY.

SEPTEMBER

MONDAY

9

TUESDAY

10

WEDNESDAY

11

PATRIOT DAY

THURSDAY

12

FRIDAY

13

SATURDAY/SUNDAY

14/15

PARTING IS SUCH SWEET SORROW.

SEPTEMBER

MONDAY

16

TUESDAY

17

WEDNESDAY

18

THURSDAY

19

FRIDAY

20

SATURDAY/SUNDAY

21/22

WHAT A PIECE OF WORK IS MAN.

SEPTEMBER

MONDAY

23

TUESDAY

24

WEDNESDAY

25

THURSDAY

26

FRIDAY

27

SATURDAY/SUNDAY

28/29

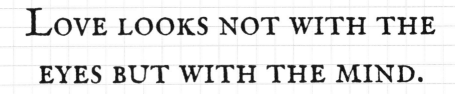

LOVE LOOKS NOT WITH THE EYES BUT WITH THE MIND.

SEPTEMBER/OCTOBER

MONDAY 30

TUESDAY 1

WEDNESDAY 2

THURSDAY 3

FRIDAY 4

SATURDAY/SUNDAY 5/6

SOMETHING IS ROTTEN IN THE STATE OF DENMARK.

OCTOBER

MONDAY

7

TUESDAY

8

WEDNESDAY

9

THURSDAY

10

FRIDAY

11

SATURDAY/SUNDAY

12/13

THE FAULT, DEAR BRUTUS, IS NOT IN OUR STARS.

OCTOBER

MONDAY
14

TUESDAY
15

WEDNESDAY
16

THURSDAY
17

FRIDAY
18

SATURDAY/SUNDAY
19/20

SWEETEST DAY

NEITHER A BORROWER NOR A LENDER BE.

OCTOBER

MONDAY

21

TUESDAY

22

WEDNESDAY

23

THURSDAY

24

FRIDAY

25

SATURDAY/SUNDAY

26/27

How sharper than a serpent's tooth it is to have a thankless child!

OCTOBER/NOVEMBER

MONDAY

28

TUESDAY

29

WEDNESDAY

30

THURSDAY

31

HALLOWEEN

FRIDAY

1

SATURDAY/SUNDAY

2/3

GET THEE TO A NUNNERY.

NOVEMBER

MONDAY	**4**
TUESDAY	**5**
WEDNESDAY	**6**
THURSDAY	**7**
FRIDAY	**8**
SATURDAY/SUNDAY	**9/10**

THE BETTER PART OF VALOUR IS DISCRETION.

NOVEMBER

MONDAY

11

VETERANS' DAY

TUESDAY

12

WEDNESDAY

13

THURSDAY

14

FRIDAY

15

SATURDAY/SUNDAY

16/17

I come to bury Caesar, not to praise him.

NOVEMBER

MONDAY **18**

TUESDAY **19**

WEDNESDAY **20**

THURSDAY **21**

FRIDAY **22**

SATURDAY/SUNDAY **23/24**

Nothing will come of nothing.

NOVEMBER/DECEMBER

MONDAY
25

TUESDAY
26

WEDNESDAY
27

THURSDAY
28

THANKSGIVING

FRIDAY
29

SATURDAY/SUNDAY
30/1

LORD, WHAT FOOLS THESE MORTALS BE!

DECEMBER

MONDAY **2**

TUESDAY **3**

WEDNESDAY **4**

THURSDAY **5**

FRIDAY **6**

SATURDAY/SUNDAY **7/8**

A HORSE! A HORSE! MY KINGDOM FOR A HORSE!

DECEMBER

MONDAY

9

TUESDAY

10

WEDNESDAY

11

THURSDAY

12

FRIDAY

13

SATURDAY/SUNDAY

14/15

OFF WITH HIS HEAD!

DECEMBER

MONDAY 16

TUESDAY 17

WEDNESDAY 18

THURSDAY 19

FRIDAY 20

SATURDAY/SUNDAY 21/21

MISERY ACQUAINTS A MAN WITH STRANGE BEDFELLOWS.

DECEMBER

MONDAY

23

TUESDAY

24

WEDNESDAY

25

CHRISTMAS

THURSDAY

26

BOXING DAY

FRIDAY

27

SATURDAY/SUNDAY

28/29

WE HAVE SEEN BETTER DAYS.

DECEMBER/JANUARY

MONDAY

30

TUESDAY

31

NEW YEAR'S EVE

WEDNESDAY

1

NEW YEAR'S DAY

THURSDAY

2

FRIDAY

3

SATURDAY/SUNDAY

4/5

NOTES TO THY SELF:

NOTES TO THY SELF:

NOTES TO THY SELF:

NOTES TO THY SELF:

THANKS FOR USING THE 2019 SHAKES-PLANNER.
I HOPE YOU ENJOYED THE SHAKESPEARE QUOTES THAT I
PICKED OUT FOR YOU THROUGHOUT THE YEAR.

MY WEBSITE IS:
WWW.PLAYONWORDSDESIGN.COM

CONNECT WITH ME ON SOCIAL MEDIA -
I'D LOVE TO HEAR FROM YOU.
FACEBOOK.COM/POWONWHEELS
INSTAGRAM.COM/POWONWHEELS
PINTEREST.COM/POWONWHEELS
TWITTER.COM/POWONWHEELS

EMAIL ME: POWONWHEELS@GMAIL.COM

THANKS AGAIN!
KELLY SCHAUB / PLAY ON WORDS DESIGN

Printed in Great Britain
by Amazon